This Is a Dream

One Lonely Boy's Story

By

Larry D. Keiser

ISBN: 1-40332-133-7

This book is printed on acid free paper.

1st Books - rev. 05/23/02

Dedication

This story is dedicated to all abused children... girls or boys. Most people refuse to acknowledge child abuse – those who do, think mainly of abusive fathers and abused little girls. There are more abused little boys than anyone knows. It is not "manly" to admit such things, so they are not admitted.

I hope one of the gifts resulting from sharing this story is for men and boys to be a little less "macho" and tell their own stories. Men need to learn to feel... not feeling is not being truly alive.

"Henry" is obviously not his real name. His story, the feelings, the hurts are real.

This effort is also dedicated to my wife and partner, Mari and to Mrs. Marcella O'Connor who discovered the writer in me. Finally, this effort is dedicated to a certain German Shepherd who will never be forgotten.

CHAPTER ONE

An old Dodge panel truck speeds along a dirt road high on a cliff overlooking the east side of the city. At the wheel is a little boy. The little boy is fighting to control the truck while at the same time battling the urge to turn right off the cliff.

The truck's speed increases and the little boy is tossed around in the cab using all of his strength to hold onto the old steering wheel. Finally, the urge becomes too strong and he turns the huge steering wheel violently to the right. The old truck plunges into the blackness of the night, whirling and turning as it falls. The little boy is terrified! He can almost see the horrible end he is falling toward... he calls out for help... but none is available to him. Suddenly he remembers the key to surviving his predicament.

All he has to do is say "this is a dream," out loud, then it will all go away. It is hard for him to say it... it is as if someone doesn't want him to stop his fall. He tries to call out.

Finally, he says something out loud and as if to trick someone he quickly yells: "This is a dream!!!!" Abruptly the little boy is no longer falling in the truck, but is being held prisoner by unseen but terrifying captors in a tunnel full of swirling darkness, putrid smells, awful noises and grotesque colors. As he is suspended he can see nothing but turmoil; and yet he can hear voices and feel burning pain and searing heat... what has he done?

Then it is over. The little boy awakes gasping for breath and stares toward the ceiling and then the walls.

Yes, he is in his room... or is he? No, this is the downstairs room at Grandma and Grandpa's. It is all right. He can go back to sleep again.

The dream repeats several times during the night, but each time the little boy yells: "This is a dream!!!!" loudly and escapes through the terrible tunnel.

In the morning he awakes and goes into the bathroom. There is no hot water in the house, but he is used to washing in cold. The shock of the cold water also helps him to gain full consciousness. "What is going to happen today?" he thinks to himself.

The little boy's grandmother is a frail and sickly looking woman in her seventies. She has a severe heart condition and looks much older than she really is. She gives her grandson his breakfast of one ounce of dry cereal and a half glass of skimmed milk. It is obvious she isn't happy with this task. She would rather give the boy a big healthy breakfast, but she knows she can't do it.

"Good morning, Grandma." says the boy. "Good morning, Henry," she returns.

"You'd better hurry, you have to be ready to go to school," she admonishes.

Henry thought for a moment about school. His experiences in the night haunted him so much that he had to think about things like school on purpose. "Oh that's alright, grandma, I have plenty of time. The bus won't be here for a long time," he says as he begins to warm to the heat of the kitchen, and the old woman's love.

"Henry! You know better than that! You don't ride a bus any more. What's wrong with you?" she was frustrated, but could almost understand the boy's confusion. This was the third school he had attended since this school year began.

Franklin Roosevelt School was different than any other school Henry had attended. In this school there were many different kinds of kids. There were Negroes and funny talking white kids; and there were the others. Henry wasn't sure what to call them. The other kids called them "gimps" or "cripples", but he didn't like those names. Besides, even the teachers thought he was one of them when he first started school here.

After the "Pledge of Allegiance" and "the Lord's Prayer", the teacher called on each kid to come forward and give his multiplication tables.

Henry had really meant to study the night before, but the events of the evening had made it impossible. Henry thought that he might explain to the teacher; but he knew she wouldn't believe him—no one ever believed him. Fear filled him as the others went forward. Each time they made a mistake the teacher rapped her ruler across their little hands held firmly on her desk. Each time a mistake was made and the teacher's corrective swat was administered, Henry felt the pain along with the other kid. He also knew that if the hands were moved and the teacher missed, the kid would have to bend over for a real spanking! He fought back the tears as his name was called. At first he pretended not to hear his name, but Mrs. O'Reilly just screamed at him... and he couldn't ignore that. So he got up from his desk and walked up to the teacher's desk. As he walked he could feel the eyes of the class on him. He could hear what they always said about him. He was so fat and stupid. "He should of stayed with the gimps downstairs where he belonged."

When he was in the other classroom, he was comfortable. The teachers were nice and they asked him to do some pretty funny things like writing his name with a big pencil wrapped in both fists; but he could do that easily. What he didn't like was the day his grandmother and mother came to the school because he didn't belong with those "retards" and "crips". That day everyone was mad at him and he got yelled at or hit by just about everyone! The principal said it was his fault because of the way he looked and acted. His mother said he looked the way he did because of a thyroid condition and his grandmother volunteered that he just acted stupid because he was shy. Henry didn't know what to do or think... he just knew he was going to get it. And, he did. His thoughts came back to today as he placed his hands on Mrs. O'Rielly's desk.

The welts on the backs of his hands were still visible when he got home from school. Henry had never learned anything through these methods and he was sure he didn't like them one bit. He thought how the teachers were nicer in the other schools he had attended across town. The teachers were nicer, but the kids were horrible! At least in this neighborhood he knew all kinds of the kids. He and the other kids seemed to have a lot in common; but he didn't know exactly what it was.

He gave his grandmother a big hug and went out on the porch to watch for his Grandpa to come home from work. Henry's Grandpa was a tall dark and powerful man. He was the same age as his grandmother, but looked young enough to be one of her sons. That really made Henry's Grandma angry when people said something about it, too! Henry's grandfather had been a "teamster" back when that meant driving horses. He drove the first motorized truck in the town and was always talking about how things used to be. Henry loved his grandfather's stories especially because of the man telling them, he knew they were absolutely true. Henry wanted to be like his grandfather. He wanted to look like his grandfather and drive trucks, but most of all he wanted people to believe him, too.

Once his grandparents were both home Henry felt comfortable for the first time that day. He could now go into his downstairs room and study those darned multiplication tables. He didn't want to be "thwapped" across the back of the hands on the teacher's desk the next day.

During the evening the police came to the house next door again. Henry hoped Melvin and Marvin's mother's boyfriend was taken away because the guy beat them and ate all the food in the house. They were mostly scared when he had been drinking... and that was most of the time. The police were common visitors to the neighborhood... so were the firemen. Henry always wondered if they had policemen and firemen on the other side of town where he lived with his mom most of the time.

This time Melvin and Marvin's mother came screaming out of the house. Her sobs were so deep, Henry immediately began to cry, too, even though he didn't know why. Henry's grandpa went over to the Washington's house after the police left. The Washington's owned the house next door. They were really nice people and never made Henry feel bad. Their daughters were very pretty and Henry often imagined Mary Ann as his girl friend. Melvin and

Marvin's mother rented the room on the west side of the Washington's house.

Grandpa came back and told Henry to sit down. Henry knew something was wrong.

"Henry, I just talked to Mr. Washington next door. He explained that the police were there to tell Miss Brown that her son, Marvin had died," explained Henry's grandfather.

"What happened?!?!?" asked Henry as the tears began to flow again.

"He dove off the high diving board at the beach into water that was too shallow—he broke his neck," said Grandpa.

"But he can't die! He is one of my only friends!" protested Henry.

"It was his time, Henry. We never know when it is our time to go. God needed Marvin to help him or it

11

wouldn't have happened," explained Henry's grandfather... "And, besides, Henry, I want you to be friends with the white children in the neighborhood," added Henry's grandmother.

"I don't care—he was my friend," sobbed Henry.

"Now stop that, Henry! Stop it right now! It is almost time for your mother to get home. You don't want her to see you like this do you?" the grandmother said knowing she had used magic words.

Henry fought back the tears and prepared for his mother's arrival. He went up the stairs with his grandma, gave her a kiss goodnight and climbed over the transom into his "upstairs" room. Grandma closed the door, but not so tight that he didn't have any light.

CHAPTER TWO

Henry's "upstairs room" was the worst place in the whole world as far as he was concerned. It seemed everything that ever went in there— died there!

His parakeet, "Ike" was dead in his cage one day last week when Henry got home from school. His mother's boyfriend said it was the heat and that birds needed light to live. Henry felt bad that he had killed his pet. His two baby turtles had died in there, too. It was a bad place.

The room was really one end of the old house's attic. Torn and faded curtains marked the end of the flooring boards about half way across the small attic. There was a window in the gable at the far end, but it never offered much light. At night Henry would hear noises. His grandpa told him they were squirrels, but Henry had seen them and they didn't have bushy tails... and some of them flew, but then he had heard something about flying squirrels so maybe his grandpa was right.

Henry's bed was a roll-away. He liked that much better than the old Army cot he used to sleep on, but he liked his real bed on the other side of town best of all! When he lived over there he had a real room with nice furniture. He didn't understand about money problems, but he knew that was part of the reason he and his mother were living with his grandparents this time.

His "downstairs" bedroom was where he slept when he stayed with his grandparents... on weekends, or when his mother was in trouble or gone. It was not as nice as his bedrooms on the other side of town, but it was by far the most comfortable place he ever stayed.

Now that his mother lived there, too, he had to sleep in his "upstairs" bedroom. At least when his mother was going to be around. Other times he could talk his grandmother into to letting him sleep downstairs.

At night Henry listened to the trains rolling by just across the river. Their noises had been his lullaby over the years and usually made him fall asleep, but that was in his "downstairs" bedroom... that was different. Here there were other noises and scary feelings and funny smells. Here he was always afraid. Afraid that he wasn't alone... or that he was alone, he wasn't sure... he just didn't like that room! It seemed like hours when he heard his mother climbing the stairs. Then he heard his grandma talking with his mother. Just as an argument was starting a man's voice interrupted. Henry had never heard this one before, but he knew it was one of his mother's boyfriends.

15

As the couple reached the place almost all the way up the stairs where the door to Henry's "upstairs" room was his mother hollered: "You'd better be asleep in there!" And then Henry heard the door squeak as the last rays of light disappeared... then he heard the latch on the outside of the door.

"Are you sure that thing is your kid, Gwen?" asked the stranger's voice.

"Yeah, it's mine alright. He takes after his father's side of the family," she explained.

"But I saw him last weekend and he is so huge," the man's voice continued.

"He has a thyroid condition, that's all. Hey, are you here to talk about that mistake or to have some fun?" she said as the voices moved into her bedroom across the kitchen from Henry's "upstairs" room.

The voices got louder again after a while, but Henry couldn't understand what they were saying or why they were yelling and making strange noises. He had heard those noises before, but couldn't remember much except that he was skinny then. By this time Henry realized he had to go to the bathroom. There was a chamber pot by his bed, but he hated the smell afterwards. Did he dare ask to be let out of his room to go to the bathroom?

He called out: "Mommy, may I please go to the bathroom downstairs?"

"I knew you weren't asleep! I told you to be asleep by the time I got home! Your grandmother is ruining you! You used to know how to mind, you big bastard!" she screamed.

"But I gotta go bad..." he began to plead.

"I said NO! Use the chamber pot!!" his mother yelled.

"But I didn't hear you say No. You said I should be asleep and…" He was cut off by the man's voice.

"Your mother said NO and that's that… use the pot if you have to go so bad."

Henry dared not say anything else. He also knew he was going to have to pee so they could hear him, but he couldn't now. If he didn't pee they would never believe him. Henry pushed as hard as he could and finally the stream started.

CHAPTER THREE

The walls of the room looked funny. Then he noticed the fire between the boards. This wasn't his bedroom. Henry cried out, but no one came. The flames were inside the room now and he was feeling both cold and hot at the same time. Henry realized this wasn't his home at all... this was HELL, and he was finally there. Then he saw scary creatures and other people... mean looking people. They saw him and came to him and started to touch him like his mother used to. "I've died and gone to hell! Can't somebody help me?" the terror struck the little boy through.

"I know I've been bad, but I'll try harder. Give me another chance, please!! I'm sorry!! I'm very sorry!!!" cried Henry.

"Is this a dream?" he yelled and suddenly he was in the tunnel and scared even more. This time it didn't end. He was back in the flames and the people were touching him... he was hot and cold... and then hot again. The flames engulfed him and then he was alone.

This time he felt like he was floating, the color was red, but there were no more flames and he didn't feel hot... he felt very cold. He felt jabs of pain. He could hear voices, but couldn't understand them. He was inside something and couldn't get out. He was trapped.

Then Henry recognized that he had been here before. He yelled, "THIS IS A DREAM!" He was swirled into the awful tunnel... and then it was morning.

Henry awoke sweating. He started to focus. "Where am I?" Then he could see he was in his "downstairs" bedroom. As thoughts began to replace fear in his head, he realized it was Wednesday.

Wednesday used to be Henry's favorite day. Henry's daddy use to pick him up after school and they would go to a movie together. He liked that. Afterwards his dad would deliver him to his grandparent's house and say: "See you on the weekend!"

One Wednesday Henry's dad had stopped by the music store where he worked to pick up something. Henry liked the music store. He wanted to learn to play the trumpet. His dad taught accordion. Henry hated accordion, but that was all he was allowed to play so he tried his best. He wasn't very good though and his dad finally gave up. Henry was looking at the trumpets in the glass case when the front door exploded. The burglar alarm went off and through the noise he could hear his mother screaming at him. "I knew you were sneaking around behind my back!" she screamed. "You little liar, I can't trust you out of my sight," she continued.

By this time Henry could see a policeman and his dad who had entered the main room of the store from the basement where he had been looking for some papers. Everybody was screaming and Henry got scared and began to cry.

"Shut up you big ugly baby!" his mother warned. "I'll kick the livin' shit out of you if you don't stop that ballin'!!" Henry knew he had better fight back the tears. Henry was knocked off his feet and was being dragged behind his mother when the policeman helped him up and stopped his mother at the door.

"Look, Ma'am, I told you to wait with me for the store manager. You are responsible for this broken door and..." the officer was interrupted by Henry's father. "It's OK, officer, I work here. I'll take care of the door when Mr. Rhoades gets here," he said.

"Thank you. I'm sorry about all this, but she showed me the papers and I had no choice," the officer said apologetically. "I understand, officer. This is not new to me," said Henry's father.

By then Henry was in his mother's brand new 1954 Oldsmobile 98 Holiday two door hardtop and on his way to his grandma and grandpa's house.

"I'm leaving this kid here because I have to go back to work, but I'm warning you... don't let that bastard of a father pick him up any day but Saturday night after five. That's what the court says and that's the way it will be!" She didn't wait for an answer. That night Henry slept in the "downstairs" bedroom.

CHAPTER FOUR

PAIN, WHITE LIGHT, LIKE LIGHTNING ALL AROUND, SCREAMING, HURT, BLOOD, MORE PAIN... the air was charged with electricity as it turned red, then orange, then white with rage as he was being beaten, kicked, scratched. It was a furious vortex swirling around him, but he knew he could stop it all if he could just say the words. He started to scream: "This is a dr—," but his mother's hand slapped over his mouth and he was told to shut up or he would get worse! Henry had hoped it was just a dream, but he knew better now. He knew he had to take what he deserved. He tried to think what he had done wrong, but he couldn't think of anything but the way he felt. Then he was down on the floor... it was almost over now. A final kick and it was over. He waited for a while and then went downstairs to clean himself up.

He was careful not to disturb his grandparents. If they found out he would be in even more trouble. He tried before to tell them, but things just got worse. He cried in the bathroom until the sun peeked into the window. It was time to get ready for school.

School was no better than usual, but it was Friday and Henry liked Fridays. This was to be an unusual Friday for Henry.

Normally Henry went to the auction barn with his grandparents and then came home to watch "Friday Night Fights" with them; but tonight his mother was home. She said something about suspended or something, but that her union steward would fix things for her or else he'd have to get his "jollys" from someone else.

It is surprising how much an eight year old understands that adults think he doesn't. Henry knew all about "jollys". His mother used to say that is what she and Henry were doing back on the other side of town.

Henry used to want to be close to his mother, but now he felt guilty because he felt better when she wasn't around. Henry knew he was wrong to think that way, but he just couldn't help it.

Henry's mother had fixed yams for dinner. Henry hated yams. He took a bite and it kind of "stuck" in his throat and choked him. His mother yelled at him to swallow it or he couldn't have his half glass of water. Henry tried, but the harder he tried... the worse it felt. Then he spit it out. It was like the fire and swirling of his nightmares. It was like the room exploded into red flames and hot winds. His mother was enraged.

"Eat that or I'll kick the shit out of you!" she screamed.

"I can't, I'm sorry but I just can't," Henry cried.

"Stop that crying or I'll give you something to cry about!" his mother returned.

"Please, mother, may I just go to bed?" he pleaded.

"NO! I said eat that and that's what you will do or else. Don't defy me you worthless bastard," she yelled.

"I'm sorry, but I just can't, Mother," he sobbed. His mother grabbed her special broom that she used to punish him. The broom was thicker than a normal broom. The handle was about an inch and a half thick.

She hit him on the knee, which was one of her favorite targets, but Henry just stood there and began to think about other things as he usually did during these beatings. He could delay the feeling of pain and avoid hearing the awful things she said... as long as the air

27

stayed red. Now the air turned white and the swirling rage was like the tornado in the movie "Wizard of Oz".

His mother quit hitting him on the legs and back and swung with all her might, laying the thick broom handle across the side of Henry's head. The broom handle broke with a loud crack that he heard as much as felt. "Eat it!" she growled.

"I can't," he cried.

"That's it. I've had it with your obstinacy. You're gonna learn just who is your boss," she said as she grabbed Henry with one hand and grabbed the broken broom handle with the other.

"What are you going to do?" screamed Henry knowing all too well that he had been really BAD this time. Henry's face was pushed to the floor with his hind end stuck up in the air. He heard the sound of his pants ripping more than he felt it. He tried to get loose, but his mother stepped on his head and then he felt the pain of the broken broom handle being shoved up his rear end. He broke loose and reached for the broom handle, but it hurt too much and he couldn't reach it anyway.

His mother pulled up his torn pants and cuddled him as if she had just kissed him goodnight instead of hurting him. Then she opened the door to his upstairs bedroom and shoved him in with her foot.

"I don't want to hear a peep out of you," she said almost calmly. "You'll stay in your room until I think you can be a good boy again," she said as she latched the door.

"Mommy please, I'll be good. What did I do so bad? Can I take this out now? Oh please, Mommy," Henry cried out.

"I told you to shut up, you fat, worthless slob," his mother said coldly.

Henry fought against the mass of his own body to reach the broom handle. He was feeling funny and thought he was having an accident in his pants. He finally reached the broom handle and pulled it out. He knew he would be hurt again if his mother knew he removed it, but she was talking with someone now and never came back after she locked him in his "upstairs" room. Henry knew he was wrong in doing it, but it hurt so... he did it anyway. He couldn't see anything, but he knew he was a mess, so he slept on the floor that night so he wouldn't mess up his bed and get into trouble for that. The next morning he quietly pushed on the door to see if it was unlocked. He heard a couple of screws fall onto the stairs and then the latch squeaked as it slid down the frame of the door and the daylight streamed in.

He grabbed some clothes and sneaked down the stairs to the bathroom. He put some water into the tub and took off the clothes he had slept in. He tried to rinse them out, but they were a mess. It wasn't diarrhea as he thought it was... it was blood. Henry cleaned himself up, put on his clothes and sneaked out to the garbage can where he hid his bloody clothes. Then he went back upstairs and waited until he heard his grandma and grandpa downstairs.

"Boy, have you got a bad case of piles," his grandmother hollered. "Look at your pants!"

She took off Henry's pants, which were stained red now and cleaned him up again. He was so embarrassed he could die. He didn't say anything... he never said anything when he couldn't think of anything to say.

He could hear his grandparents talking, but he felt funny and the room started to spin around. The next thing he remembered he was laying on the sofa in the living room. He must be late for school. He tried to sit up, but he still felt very funny.

"There you are. You fainted, Henry. You must have lost a lot of blood," said his grandmother. "I've heard people built like you could get piles, but I never saw them bleed so bad on a youngster before!"

"I got to go to school," Henry said as he tried to get up again.

"No not today, Henry... it's Saturday," the old lady explained.

"Where's mother?" he asked.

"We don't know, Henry. She was rather upset last night and came downstairs to call one of her man friends. We heard him arrive and then both of them leave," explained his grandfather.

"I think your shows are on, Henry. Would you like me to turn on the TV?" his grandfather said as he reached for the television.

CHAPTER FIVE

The sky was blue with white puffy clouds and Henry felt cool and exhilarated as he swooped down toward the top of a tree. He thought the world was beautiful for the first time. He heard music. He felt the warmth of the sun on his skin and then he saw what was happening on the ground. Henry flew down toward the commotion.

A woman was yelling at a little boy. She began hitting the little boy and then a man came into view and starting kicking the little boy. Henry could watch no more! With a strength he knew he had but had never before experienced; he landed between the youngster and the adults. The adults tried to beat on him, but couldn't hurt him... he turned and grabbed the little boy and leaped into air. Henry flew away with the little boy... as he flew the little boy hugged Henry and started to say something... "Henry! Time to get up! You don't want to be late to school," it was his grandfather's voice.

It was a special day at school this day. In the afternoon Henry's class would go out to the park and have a picnic. Henry was excited about it. He knew he would have a special treat in his lunch bag.

When they got to the park the teacher led the class in a song and then they all sat down at the tables. There were hot dogs, hamburgers, cake and ice cream... all the things kids Henry's age just loved.

Henry reached into his paper sack and saw his treat. It was the best thing he had seen in weeks! It was a whole quarter of a banana! He was off his diet for the party... oh boy!! The teacher and one kid's mother tried to get Henry to eat with the other kids, but Henry said he couldn't and besides he had his treat anyway. They finally gave up and turned away, but Henry knew they were talking about him. When Henry got home that afternoon he told his grandma how good he was at the park and thanked her for the treat. She said she was proud of him, but she couldn't understand how he had so much "will-power" not to eat all that other stuff. Henry was sure his grandmother believed him about the party, but he knew nobody else would, so he didn't say anything about it to anyone else... even though it was the best, hardest good thing he had done right in a long time.

Especially because he was so good at the party he was quite proud of himself and almost looking forward to the next visit to the doctor's office. The doctor had explained one time that Henry's body didn't take care of his food the way normal bodies did. That was why he was "obese". That is why he could only have certain foods and then only small amounts of those foods. The doctor said something about six hundred calories a day, but Henry didn't understand what that meant.

This trip to the doctor's office Henry was proud of how good he had been not to take extra food... even though people offered it to him. He got proudly onto the scales and then saw the nurse writing down a number even higher than the last time. He wanted to cry, but knew he couldn't. Dr. Bernstein was Henry's favorite doctor out of all the doctors he had seen over the years. He didn't understand why they kept changing doctors all the time. Sometimes he wondered if the arguments his mother always had with the doctor had anything to do with it, but then she argued with everybody.

The doctor sounded concerned when Henry finally saw him. Dr. Bernstein finally said that he wanted Henry to take a special test. When the doctor explained that this wasn't a test Henry would be graded on he relaxed a little.

On the day of the test Henry and his mom entered a big cold building that Henry had seen before on the outside, but had never been inside before. He didn't like it. When they entered an office a couple of nurses acted like they were waiting for him and took him directly into a little room that had a big thing that looked like a can in the middle of it. They gave something to Henry to drink and then some kind of a cookie. Henry protested that he couldn't eat anything else that day if he had a cookie, but the nurse just told him to eat it and be quiet. After he finished the cookie he was told to just sit there and not do anything until they came back.

It seemed to Henry that he had been there all day when one of the nurses and a doctor he had never met... which Henry thought was impossible because he was sure he had met them all... asked him to hop up into the can. Henry couldn't make it that high and the two white-coated people finally helped. They told Henry to relax, but not to go to sleep until they told him it was all right... and then they closed the end of the can! The can that seemed so big from the outside now felt very small. Henry could move his arms and legs a little, but he could not sit up, or even move his arm under him to lean on his elbow and look out the little window. Henry first thought he understood how peaches felt... but then he began to get afraid. He didn't want to be inside a can. Then a funny sounding voice said for him to settle down or he would ruin the test. Henry didn't want to ruin the test, so he tried to settle down.

It seemed like hours had passed when the funny voice said: "Don't go to sleep!" He tried not to sleep. Then they said it was OK to sleep... he couldn't... Henry just wanted to get out of that can. He wanted that more than anything else in his whole life! He tried to push on the top, but all that happened was the funny voice said: "stop moving!" He pushed on the bottom and the voice said: "If you don't stop moving we'll have to do this whole thing again another day... well, Henry didn't want to do this ever again so he stayed as still as he could.

Henry was sure he had been in the can for several days when the doctor who put him in there opened the can and pulled him out. Henry was very happy that the

test was over!

CHAPTER SIX

Henry was back on the other side of town again. It was nice to see his buddies and play with them, but he didn't like being home with his mother. He knew he couldn't tell anybody why.

He was running around playing Korean War with his friends when his stomach hurt really bad. Suddenly it felt like his own stomach had knocked him down on the ground! He was all bent over and his buddies were yelling at him to get up. He tried but it hurt too much. As he lay there he started to cry, but knew he shouldn't so he tried to stop. He wasn't supposed to cry. That was for sissies!

Arnie's dad worked in a grocery store and he went to work later than everyone else's dad. Mr. Brawer and

Henry's two friends helped Henry to his house. The door was locked, as it was suppose to be. Henry explained that Mrs. Frederickson would be there at lunchtime to let him in to eat lunch and go to the bathroom. Mr. Brawer acted like he couldn't understand what Henry was saying. Henry just knew he hurt. This was bad!

Mr. Brawer left and came back in a few minutes. Shortly Grandma and Grandpa were there and grandpa and Mr. Brawer helped Henry into the car. Next thing Henry knew he was at the hospital again.

The doctor came in and said hello. This was a different doctor. Henry didn't like him. He smelled funny and acted like his mother's boy friends. The doctor told Henry he had to stop eating certain things. Henry started reciting his diet when the doctor interrupted and gave him a sheet of paper. He could read most of it and it was different than his other diet. He tried to explain to the new doctor, but he just told Henry that Henry just didn't understand and that he was Henry's new doctor.

The doctor and a nurse talked in the hall, but Henry could hear part of what they were saying. The doctor said something about contusions and broken bones, but Henry didn't remember falling down... in fact, he never remembered when he fell down.

Henry's mom always reminded him of his accidents. Being stupid Henry had a very bad memory. He would never remember what really happened and remembered a lot of stuff that never happened. This is how Henry knew how stupid he really was.

Then the doctor told the nurse that he was convinced Henry had an ulcer... whatever that was. The nurse couldn't believe that an eight-year-old could have an ulcer. She seemed to be crying when she came into Henry's room. People often cried when they talked to Henry... he didn't like that. He wanted to cry... not make other people cry. Days and nights in the hospital always felt the same. Henry just lay there and wished he were somewhere else. His daddy stopped in one day and asked Henry if there was anything he wanted. Henry said he wanted a big red fire engine, but his daddy said he couldn't afford that... was there anything else. Henry said he'd like an orange then. His daddy also said that Henry would be living with his grandparents again and that his mother was going to be living there again, too. He said his mother had sold their house and that he was very upset, but that part of the money would help Henry go to school.

CHAPTER SEVEN

It was the end of the longest school year Henry could remember. He had had the meetings with the school nurse, his teacher, the principal and his mother... just like every year... and he passed... just barely.

People were always telling him he was lazy and that he just didn't do as well as they knew he could in school. They said with his I. Q. he should get all A's and maybe even skip a grade or two, but that he just didn't apply himself. He had heard that same talk a thousand times before. All Henry knew was that the worst school year of his life was over! He had been to three different schools this year and each time he moved... the school got worse! This last teacher Mrs. Hagstrom was really tough!

Anyway it was all through and Henry figured he would be at a different school in the fall anyway... it was summertime! Henry met his Chinese friend, Lin, that morning to play. They were going to play at the schoolyard when they saw their teacher. She was carrying some heavy boxes. Henry didn't like her at all. She never listened to him and was always telling him he couldn't do things he knew he could do... if he had a little more time. BUT, he was taught to always be a gentleman... and his grandpa always told him to do nice things for the people you dislike most... and you may learn to like them. So, he convinced Lin to ask Mrs. Hagstrom if they could help.

Mrs. Hagstrom looked very surprised to see Henry and Lin and thought a minute before she finally said;

"Ok, boys, I'll give you each a dime if you help me sort these books and put them in my car." Henry said; "We don't need no money, we just want to help." He realized he said what he did wrong, and was very surprised he didn't get corrected. It took all morning to do the work she had the boys do. Henry was sure that all that work was worth more than a dime, but then he liked the different way Mrs. Hagstrom looked at him all that morning so it was worth it.

After the boys had finished and said good bye to their teacher they decided to play Army in the old house behind Lin's house. The boys played for a while and then Lin's mother called to him and yelled about not playing in the house that was going to be torn down.

The boys had been waiting for months to see the men come and knock it down with a steam shovel, but they hadn't done it yet so they used the old house as a playhouse. Lin's mother put up such a fuss that they decided they had better find somewhere else to play.

As they ran away from the old house they ran by the foundation of another building that had been torn down already. Henry slipped and fell down. Just as he hit the ground, Lin's father's dog charged Henry and grabbed his leg in his mouth. Lin yelled at the dog and Henry screamed at the pain. Blood was squirting all over. The dog backed off chewing on a big piece of meat. Henry wondered where the meat had come from... and then noticed another piece of meat laying—or hanging on his leg.

He tried to shake the meat off his leg so the dog wouldn't grab him again. But, the meat just hung there and Henry was having trouble moving at all. Then he

Larry D. Keiser

noticed that blood was squirting out like water out of a garden hose, Henry knew he had to get home.

Henry's grandma had had several heart attacks before. She had them right on the sidewalk downtown and Henry just got her medicine for her and sat by her waiting and watching to see if he needed to call a policeman. She always got up after a while and they would go into a dime store and sit at the lunch counter until she felt good enough to go home.

This time he was in trouble, too. He felt bad because he knew he had caused the heart attack. He was trying to get her medicine and bleeding all over. She was having a heart attack and spilling Mercurochrome all over the place.

Finally Henry grabbed the phone and asked the operator to get the police for him. When the policeman answered, Henry said, "Tell Chief Ruger Henry called and my grandma is having a heart attack..." Henry could say no more. Chief Ruger and his wife and daughter were friends of his parents and Henry's too. Henry's grandma always told Henry that Chief Ruger and Mrs. Ruger would be Henry's God Parents, if he had God Parents.

As he was putting the phone down he heard the siren, within a couple of minutes the car pulled up in front, then another, then the chief himself. Henry wished he could watch what was going on, but he felt really funny and he was worried about Grandma. She was sitting on the couch as a policeman wrapped up Henry's leg and then they took him to the hospital. Henry had always wanted to ride in a police car, but this trip was no fun at all. Henry was beginning to feel hurt... this was worse than any of his falls.

The bleeding was almost stopped. Now Henry was beginning to hurt so bad that the air in the room changed colors. Then his mother came into the room and she starting yelling at Henry for causing her to lose work. She yelled and screamed at Henry until a nurse took Henry into the treatment room. The nurse called Henry's mom a bad name. Henry had wanted to call her that, but didn't dare. The police officer pushed his mom into a chair and told her he wanted to talk to her some more. The doctor came in (another new one Henry had never seen before) and cut the meat that was hanging out of Henry's leg and started sewing up the wound. When the sewing was finished Henry and his mom went to the desk. The doctor asked Henry's mom a lot of questions and seemed upset by her answers. Then the doctor offered Henry a sucker for being such a brave boy.

"You can't give that obese monster candy... you idiot! What kind of a doctor do you think you are? I'm going to report you to the hospital administrator..." Henry's mother protested.

"No thank you doctor. I don't feel too good. Things look funn-..." Henry said as he passed out.

As Henry woke up, he was looking at the bright light and Henry's mom was talking about plastic surgery with the doctor. She was saying that someone who looked like Henry was a waste to spend money for plastic surgery on. The doctor explained that Henry's leg would look strange as he had lost several muscles to the dog. She said that would be his best leg because it wouldn't look so fat. Then they noticed Henry was awake.

Henry had to use crutches in order to get around. They hurt his armpits almost as much as his leg hurt.

They also made him take medicine that made him have funny dreams. Some of those dreams happened when Henry was sure he was awake... but then again, Henry was told he daydreamed a lot anyway. A day or two later Chief Ruger came to Henry's grandparent's house to talk with Henry's mother. "Oh, what now?" she asked.

He explained that the dog that had Henry for lunch had died. Henry felt really bad... was he so bad that he killed a dog!?! Chief Ruger said that Lin's father had buried the dog, but the police dug him up and that he had rabies. Henry had no idea what rabies was. When he found out it meant a lot of shots, he knew he didn't like rabies at all!

It was hard for Henry to get around, but some of his friends would stop by and talk to him or try to play while Henry was stuck on the porch. Henry became concerned that Lin never came over. One of his friends explained that Lin hated Henry because his father told him that Henry's grandfather had poisoned their dog. Henry knew his Grandpa would never do a thing like that. He knew he had killed the dog.

CHAPTER EIGHT

Henry loved the woods. He was glad his mom and her husband had moved up north so Henry could spend time in the woods. There had been many moves, but that all changed and they had been in this house for a long time. Henry didn't have a lot of friends, but since he was beginning to slim down, he had a new best friend, David.

Most of the other kids didn't like David. They said things about him that other kids used to always say about Henry. Henry didn't like people who said those things. He thought David was about the neatest kid he had ever met! David's father could fly airplanes and he had a ranch. It didn't matter to Henry that it was a mink ranch... Sky King had a ranch and flew airplanes so David's father had to be a neat guy.

David was bigger than most kids. He was taller than anyone else in school... taller than some of the teachers, even! David's mom was real nice, too. She listened when Henry talked. David had two brothers, but Henry just ignored them... just like David did. Henry wished he could be like David.

Henry and David would spend the whole summer playing in the woods. They were Air Force Pilots or Space Cadets or Soldiers. Sometimes they would be Hell Drivers and jump their bicycles over ramps they built... just like the Thrill Show drivers did on TV.

That winter there was a lot of snow! There was so much snow that the huge plows only plowed where they thought the roads were. The mailman just stuck the mail in the snow bank and everyone had bright orange balls on their car radio antennas!

Henry and David built two huge snow forts that winter—one for each of them. Then they had snow wars making lots of snowballs and snow grenades and then having great snow battles!

They also built an igloo that was big enough for both of them and Henry slept in it several times that winter. Henry really liked the solitude of the igloo.

Where Henry lived the big lake was only a half-mile away. When they first moved up north their house was right on the big lake, but they left that one and moved to this one. This house was not as fancy as the houses Henry was used to living in, but he didn't care. Henry just loved the woods and having a friend.

Near the beginning of the next school year Henry was out of school a lot. He went with his mom and step dad to see his grandma almost every day—even though it took over 2 hours to get there. It was a long boring trip even in his mom's new '57 Olds 98. Henry's step dad would really haul! That was the fastest car Henry had ever been in!

On one of those trips, Rex didn't go with Henry and his mom. As they were sailing down the road, Henry's mom said to watch as she was going to hit a big box that was in the middle of the road. Henry had a weird feeling and yelled at his mom not to do it!

Henry's mom never listened to him and gave him a nasty glance, but at the last minute she swerved the big Oldsmobile around the box in the middle of the road. Just then two small children who probably lived in the farmhouse near the road came running out of the box like there was a bear chasing them! Henry's mom slammed on the brakes! The car lurched toward the ditch. As the car came to a stop Henry saw the look in

his mother's eyes. He had never seen that look before,

but he would again very soon.

CHAPTER NINE

This was the first funeral Henry had ever been to. He didn't much like it. It seemed everyone there felt like he felt. He had always wanted someone to know how he felt, but now he was sure he didn't want that anymore.

Henry's grandmother just lay there in the fancy box. Henry couldn't understand why she didn't answer him. He asked if he should get her medicine, but his grandpa said it was too late for medicine and that Henry's grandma would never need it again and that she was not really there, but in a better place. That made Henry feel better... a little better.

At the funeral Henry's relatives kept talking about how Henry was spoiled by the old lady in the casket and how he wasn't really a relative because his mother was adopted... whatever that meant. It was then that Henry saw the look in his mom's face again. She looked empty!

The conversation made Henry feel like he didn't belong. Henry did know how it felt not to belong... he felt that way all the time.

Losing his Grandmother was a bigger change than Henry imagined. He spent less time in his hometown now. He also didn't get any new clothes anymore.

Things were getting better at school. Henry was at this one a lot longer than usual!

Henry didn't have a lot of friends, but some of the teachers seemed to like him. He joined the Boy Scouts and really liked it! He worked hard and earned his ranks quickly. He soon caught up with the other boys his age in rank and became the troop bugler and eventually a Patrol Leader. He was even chosen by his fellow Scouts to become a member of the "Order of the Arrow"!

Henry also discovered sports. He was a terrible baseball player, but he still played. He was not very good at gymnastics and hurt himself a lot, but Henry was never afraid of pain. His best sport was football.

One evening after football practice Henry was taking a long shower and realized that he was alone in the locker room! The door locked from the outside and he was locked in! Henry dressed and waited a while, but then he decided that he didn't want to spend the night in that smelly old locker room! He put on his shoulder pads and his helmet and charged the door like it was a halfback. He hit the door at full tilt and it gave way just like the halfback always did!

As he lay on the steps that led to the subterranean locker room amid the dust and wood splinters, he looked up and saw the assistant football coach standing at the top of the stairs. "I noticed you weren't on the athletic bus and was coming back to get you," his coach explained. "That was one hell of a hit!" he continued. "We'll take this up with the janitor. I think you're going to learn some carpentry young man."

The next morning in homeroom the assistant football coach who was also his home room teacher was calling roll call. When he came to Henry's name he said: "King Kong." Henry didn't answer. Mr. Vander Pohl repeated: "King Kong!" Henry, that's your new name. You know why," he said and Henry responded, "Here."

The nickname would stay with him for the rest of his time at that school. Nobody called him Henry anymore, and that was OK with him, because he didn't like the sound of his name anymore anyway.

Each night Henry would wash his slacks and shirt. He took very good care of his clothes, but after a few months they looked pretty sad. The kids at school started saying things about how they always knew what "Kong" would look like and his health class teacher wrote a message on the blackboard one day and said that it was for everybody, but especially for one person who would know who they were. The blackboard said: "Clothes do not make the man. But, they can surely un-make him!"

When Henry spent time with his grandparents before his Grandma died; he would help with the "projects" his Grandma would start. She raised chickens, hunting dogs, hamsters, birds... all kinds of animals and sold them. She always said that if Henry helped, there would be money for Henry to go to college.

Henry especially enjoyed the "Chicken Project"... although he lost his taste for fowl as a result.

Henry's Grandpa was a superman to Henry. He knew everything that Henry ever wanted to know and could do everything, too. During the "Chicken Project" Grandpa would gracefully grab a chicken from the front and pick it up suddenly with a jerk. The chicken was just as suddenly dead, and could be prepared for dinner.

Henry's Grandma, on the other hand, would chase the chickens all over the yard cussing at them all the time! Henry would laugh so hard he'd have to pee!

After she caught one she'd take it over to a stump where she kept her axe. The chicken must have known what was about to happen because it would start to shed its feathers as if to convince the old lady to cook it without killing it!? Or, so Henry thought.

Finally she would swing the axe at the chicken only to have it move and miss which brought on another chorus of cussing. She used words that Henry would only understand years later... and words for which he never learned the meaning! When the fatal blow would finally arrive, grandma would lose her grip and Henry saw what the old saying meant. A chicken running around with it's head cut off was certainly a sight to behold!!

Although Henry's mom would get and spend Henry's college fund before he ever got to use it, Henry's Grandpa gave him some of it over Christmas vacation that year.

Remembering the message on the blackboard he decided to invest some of his money on clothes. The small town where Henry lived was just a half-hour drive from Port City. Henry's mom let him off at the big department store in town and Henry went in alone.

Levi's had just come out with some really neat clothes! They were bright and colorful: red, day-glow orange, day-glow green, yellow, bright blue! Henry loved the colors and bought a whole new wardrobe.

As he left the department store he remembered he needed new shoes, too. There in the window were the "coolest" shoes he had ever seen!!! Red suede!!!!

After buying the shoes and riding home he put his clothes away almost reverently. The next morning he dressed in a bright green dress shirt with day-glow orange cotton twill dress slacks and put on his bright red shoes! Nobody missed "King Kong" at school that day!

Many people disagreed with his taste, but everyone knew he had new clothes!

CHAPTER TEN

Henry awoke as the wind of a speeding car blew in his face as it went by. He was laying on the line in the middle of the highway. He wanted to move, but couldn't. He always "chickened out" before, but he wouldn't this time. He had to be brave and maybe then he could go to a better place like his grandma.

This time the car that just went by stopped and the driver came running at him screaming! Henry scrambled to his feet and ran into the woods. The driver gave up the chase. Henry found a bed of pine needles and cried himself to sleep. He was a coward... and he was alone.

Henry slept in the woods a lot. He always thought someone would come and get him, but no one ever did.

In fact, no one ever talked about it to him. Henry's step dad and mom often talked about it to each other, though. Rex wanted Gwen to put Henry in a mental hospital. She just said it wouldn't help Henry... they never helped her! Henry was just a big ugly mistake... a mistake that she would have to pay for— for the rest of her life.

During that football season, the other guys made fun of the fact that Henry had hair in places the other guys didn't. And, there were other differences that made Henry very self-conscious.

After one practice the coach talked to "Kong" about what the others guys were saying. He explained that "Kong" was maturing sooner than the others. He also asked if "Kong" would see the team doctor about it.

By this time "Kong" was very familiar with this particular doctor! He had broken both hands in one game, his nose in another, some ribs in another, and that was even before he started gymnastics!! Yes, Henry knew and would continue to know Dr. Yeoman intimately!

When he arrived at the doctor's office the nurse was looking strangely at him. Then, he was let in and sent to the doctor's office where his desk was. He wasn't weighed and he was told he didn't have to take any clothes off!?!? When the doctor entered his office he closed the door and talked about the last game for a while. Finally, the doctor asked Henry if he was taking any medicine on a regular basis. He said he was taking one pill daily and his antihistamines for the hay fever and asthma during those times of the year. The doctor took a sample of the daily medicine and looked in a big blue book.

"Henry, I would never tell you to do anything against your parent's wishes, but do you know what this medicine is?" said the doctor with a very grim expression.

"No," said Henry.

"It is a hormone. Taking this is making you mature faster than you are supposed to. I don't believe you should take any more."

Henry asked for and got a detailed explanation. The doctor knew Henry's parents socially and was not surprised that Henry was taking the hormones to "outgrow" his obesity. "Henry, you are not obese. You don't need this stuff any more."

At that moment Henry's football coach came in. The two men Henry respected more than anybody else other than his Grandpa and his Scoutmaster talked to him like he was a man. They explained that they would back Henry up if he decided to defy his parents.

Henry made his decision. Henry hadn't seen the air turn colors in quite some time! The fury of his mother's and step father's reaction was familiar, although he knew his step dad didn't understand what this was all about... he just liked to knock Henry around.

When it was over Henry's mother told him to make highballs for her and his step dad. Feeling his defiance, he declined. That night in the woods Henry began to doubt his place in the world. "Why, God? Why do I take up space? Why do I live? I can't do anything right and cause nothing but trouble... why? WHY?"... he lost consciousness.

In the little resort town where Henry spent his junior high and part of high school years there couldn't have been 1200 houses. While going to that school, Henry lived in 6 of them! He never knew for sure why they moved so much but suspected it had something to do with not paying bills. There was a lot of loneliness during those years, but some good times, too.

Henry's eighth grade science teacher liked Henry. Henry was very interested in science and strongly affected by the Russian triumph of putting "Sputnik" in orbit before the United States had a rocket capable of the same feat. Mr. Barnhart encouraged Henry to experiment and Henry worked on propulsion systems for boats and an electro-mechanical way of putting payloads in orbit. One day during this time Mr. Barnhart took Henry aside in the hall between classes.

"Henry, do you trust me?" said the teacher.

"Of course, Mr. Barnhart." Henry replied.

"I'm going to rub this stuff on your face, hands and clothes and then set you aflame..."

"You're gonna what?!?!?!?!?" Henry interrupted.

"Look here." the teacher replied. Barnhart put some of the liquid on his arm and lighted it. "See, Henry, the liquid doesn't burn. See the space between my skin and the flame?" Henry saw the space and was a little proud that Mr. Barnhart chose him for this demonstration. After being covered with the mystery liquid and waiting for Mr. Barnhart to get to the classroom, Henry ignited himself and went slowly up the stairs to the classroom.

As he went by the office he heard the school secretary scream and the principal call the fire department. Henry just went into the classroom, apologized for being late, and sat in his assigned seat.

Neither Henry nor Mr. Barnhart could hold in the laughter any longer! The kids in the room went from shock to panic as the flames burned themselves out. Mr. Barnhart then went across the hall to explain to the principal and his disheveled secretary... and the gathering of teachers who responded to the commotion. From that moment on, "King Kong" was seen in a new "light"!

Time passed and Henry made it to high school. One night after gymnastics practice Henry walked toward his house with an uneasy feeling. Over the years he had developed a sixth sense regarding the moods of his mother. He knew instinctively that this was going to be one of those nights.

Henry hated nighttime and found every excuse for staying at school. At school he was often ridiculed and regularly hurt in accidents, but his few friends were there and he felt that he was a part of the school community... if only on the fringes.

When ever his family moved into or out of a house Henry was allowed to go through the front door. Any other time he was always supposed to go through the back door. This was a family rule.

At this particular house the backdoor opened into the garage. Henry had to open the garage door and close it before he opened the door into the kitchen. Henry turned the handle and began to open the door. He saw his mother sitting in a kitchen chair facing the door. In her lap was his grandpa's old double-barreled shotgun. She raised it and pulled the first trigger.

Henry dove for the concrete floor and slammed the door as it exploded in flames and splinters. He scrambled to his feet as the second barrel discharged with a storm of metal that only brushed by him as he ran through the other garage door and toward the woods.

The next morning he waited until his parents left for work. The door was fixed and there was a fresh coat of paint on the wall near the door. He began to wonder if it wasn't another nightmare. It was getting harder to tell the dreams from the nightmares anymore... or was it reality from dreams? The incident was never mentioned. Henry camped in the woods for over a week. He'd wait until his parents were gone and enter the house to shower and get ready for school. He always dreamed that someone would come for him, but no one ever came... not even the police.

CHAPTER ELEVEN

While Henry was still in elementary school he convinced his dad to let him take trumpet lessons. After his disappointing accordion lessons, his father was reluctant. The horn teacher at the music store had more faith in Henry and convinced his dad to let Henry try.

Henry loved his horn! He did so well that his dad exchanged his old horn for a newer one... and then got Henry a brand new horn when Henry earned first chair in the school band.

Henry felt different when he was playing music. The songs they played in elementary school band were often silly, but while he was playing he became a part of the music. He wasn't a fat, ugly, clumsy, stupid kid anymore; he was the voice of his horn singing the wonderful sounds of music!

One night toward the end of the school year Henry was riding his bike home from school. As he rode over the rise in the road near his house he saw the moving van in his front yard. "Are we moving?" he asked.

"Even you should be able to figure that out, stupid," his mother retorted.

When they moved north Henry would leave the music behind. He was the bugler for Scouts, but had to sell his real horn to buy eyeglasses because he couldn't see the board at school.

When Henry visited friends he was always surprised at how messy their homes were. His home was sterile... literally! He cleaned every room every week, and his mother usually did the same room after he was done because he was such a lousy cleaner! Every surface was cleaned and disinfected.

He was also surprised that his friends didn't have many chores to do. He had to clean bathrooms every day, other rooms once a week, wash dishes, take care of the yard, wash the car, take care of the dog when they had one, do the laundry, ironing, and mix drinks for his parents and guests. This last task was particularly unpleasant for Henry. Although his mother often accused him of stealing liquor, Henry was not interested!

Not that he had never tasted the stuff; he just didn't like the taste of anything but gin, and only liked that because it reminded him of the pines. No, he had watched what the liquor did to his mother and her friends and he didn't like it at all!

It was dish washing that got him in the most trouble, however. It happened two or three times every week. After dinner Henry would immediately start washing dishes and do the best job he thought he could... only to be cussed at, yelled at and usually swatted a few times, because his mother found a speck of food... or a water spot!

No matter how bad the nights were; Henry always made it to school the next morning. School was his haven. Over the years Henry earned more friends. Especially older girls seemed to take Henry under their wings... figuratively. Patty was Henry's friend Jim's "steady". She convinced Jim and some other friends that it was time for Henry to have a date.

Henry wasn't so convinced! Henry was confused about girls. He wanted to like them, but just turned into

Jell-O inside when he was near any girl. In spite of his many protests, a date was arranged.

The girl was named Kathy. She was on the gymnastics team and seemed to like to have Henry "spotting" for her while she performed on the uneven parallel bars. It made Henry nervous to be that close, and he nearly died when he had to catch Kathy or one of the other "female types"; but he was also proud that he was considered the best "spotter" on the team. He liked being known as someone who could save other people from harm, and who knows, he might even save a life?

Many times Henry had had "mishaps" on (or off) the trampoline. He had stuck his head through the springs on more than one occasion. He had traveled off the end and landed on the cement floor and broke both of his heels. He had missed the tramp and landed on the frame more than once. Usually the same girl was spotting for him... usually she screamed and ran when he was in trouble. Henry equated "female types" with pain. One time was especially painful!

Henry was spotting for Linda as usual. Linda was very good on floor exercise and always winning on the balance beam, but quite awkward on the trampoline. Linda did a somersault and had rotated too far before she straightened out. When her feet hit the bed of the trampoline she was catapulted forward instead of upward! Henry could see that he wasn't going to be able to push her back to the trampoline so he jumped back and set himself to catch her and break her fall.

As she fell toward the cement floor, Henry braced himself and remembered that he would have to fall with her to absorb some of the impact. As she came down Henry reached up and grabbed her legs in one arm and torso in the other and then let himself fall to the floor holding her above him. As they fell his right arm hit the floor first. It landed flat from wrist to elbow. There was a muffled cracking noise that he felt more than heard. Then the rest of his body hit the floor with Linda's falling on top of his. Henry was facing east... his arm was facing west!?

He had never heard such filthy language from such a pretty girl before! She was screaming that he had caught her for a "cheap feel" and that she was going to get him kicked off the team. Meanwhile the coach arrived and pushed Linda aside as he knelt by the unappreciated hero who was in obvious pain! Coach Smith made it clear to Linda that Henry had probably saved her life and for her to take a shower and think about the way she was acting. He also directed another gymnast to call the ambulance.

Henry had dislocated his shoulder. Because the little town had no hospital, Henry was taken to the clinic. There the doctor who was also Henry's friend the team physician gave Henry a Libby's restaurant glass to squeeze as he was going to reset the joint.

The glass shattered as Henry squeezed. The shards of glass were comically stuck into Henry's hand at odd angles. The ambulance was recalled and Henry was taken to the hospital in the Port City. X-rays revealed that Henry's collarbone was also broken and the broken pieces had been scraped together as the shoulder was relocated.

Kathy was nicer than Linda, but Henry was still petrified about the date. As the time approached he begged Patty to go to Kathy's door with him. Patty, being a good sport did... and in fact rang the doorbell and talked to Kathy's parents when Henry's mouth moved but no sounds came out! As they got to Patty's father's gorgeous Buick convertible Henry opened the door for Kathy and Patty and then went around the car to sit behind Jim.

They traveled the scenic route in to the bigger city for dinner and a movie. The top was down, the air crisp and rich with the smells of spring, and the sounds of rock and roll were pulsating from the speaker in the back seat.

Henry's nervousness became panic. He was so frightened that he jumped from the moving car, rolled across the highway, and into the ditch on the far side of the road. His clothes were a disaster. He felt some abrasions and knew he'd be black and blue in the morning, but he could tell nothing important was broken. He started walking through the woods toward home. Meanwhile Kathy was so stunned and peeved that she just sat there.

As the car slowed in the Port City limits; Jim turned to ask how Henry and Kathy were doing and saw only Kathy and she was crying. He stopped the car and asked where Henry was. Kathy said he'd jumped out of the car miles back... and that she wanted to go home. By the time school started Monday morning rumors about what happened in the back seat were many.

Henry tried to apologize to Kathy and told everyone that it was his fault, she didn't do anything, but nobody believed him. Kathy refused to talk to him.

Henry was still recovering from his first date when the band director made an announcement during homeroom period one morning. He said the band needed someone to play bass horn. Henry wasn't sure what a bass horn was, but he knew he wanted to get back into band and so he volunteered. That night was his first rehearsal playing a tuba.

Henry had played other instruments, but fell in love with the wonderful low voice of the tuba! He had found his place and Henry learned the numbers they had to play at festival and did a good job by all accounts. He was truly doing what he was meant to do!

CHAPTER TWELVE

One Spring night Henry had finished his homework, done his chores and washed the dishes very carefully. His step dad didn't accuse him of watering down the drinks and his mother had even made pizza that night. Henry felt pretty good and went up stairs to listen to WLS radio from Chicago. When he got to his room, he laid on the rollaway bed that was in his room and straightened the pile of his clothes on the floor.

Until recently he had had nice bedroom furniture, but it had been sold. He hated the rollaway, but since they lived in the big city now, he couldn't sleep in the woods anymore.

This night his parents had gone out. When they returned Henry pretended to be asleep. Suddenly the light in his room came on. His mother ripped his clothes off and started to kick him in his groin and just below the knee... two of her favorite targets. His six foot three inch 225 pound stepfather held him as his mother tired herself beating on Henry's face and body.

The air turned red and then white as her rage engulfed him. When she was tired, his step dad took his turn and Henry was bleeding from his nose, mouth, ears, eyes, and later peed blood. When they were both tired they left him alone. They never told Henry why. This was the way it usually was. This was why Henry hated the night. This was not a dream, but the way Henry lived.

Henry knew he was different. He wasn't fat anymore, so he was not sure why he was always so bad. He just knew that he wanted to be somebody else... anybody else. He knew God loved other people, but just as surely he knew even God didn't like Henry. Nobody liked Henry.

Henry was never meant to be alive. He would do something someday to prove he was worthy of breathing everyone else's air. Henry dreamed of dying in some heroic rescue of someone. He wanted his death to be meaningful. He had to redeem himself for all the wrong things he had done. When he prayed for forgiveness, he was confused. He couldn't remember what he had done. He was so stupid... he couldn't even remember what he did wrong.

Henry would think about other things while his parents were punishing him. First he tried to remember what he had done that was so bad. Then he would think about his favorite songs. Then he would begin to pray. Sometimes Henry felt like someone was going to help him, but no one ever came. Henry knew he had committed some horrible sin and that he was being punished by God, too. He just couldn't remember what he did.

For a while he wanted to join a church, then the Catholic church, then the closest church... but when he would go to church, people always asked where his parents were and made him feel funny. A couple of times he heard them talking about the way he dressed. Henry thought churches were friendly places full of nice people.

He must be very evil. He must be in hell, because it sure felt like hell to him. Henry just wanted someone to hold onto him and let him cry for a while. He wanted someone to listen to him and not call him a liar. Henry was lonely. He was always lonely. Henry wanted someone to talk to. Henry had given up trying to tell anyone about his nights... no one ever believed him.

Henry didn't know why he was such a damned liar. He just knew nobody ever believed him... and he was surely damned.

CHAPTER THIRTEEN

This time Henry knew a few days in advance that they were going to move to the Port City. Henry didn't want to leave. He finally had friends, his grades were pretty good and he was back in the band. But, they moved anyway. At Port City High School Henry was overwhelmed. His school had about 300 hundred kids in four grades all under one roof. At PCHS, there were over 3,000 kids in three grades and the campus had three large buildings and three or four smaller ones!!

Henry first tried to get onto the football team. The coach just laughed. "I've got water boys bigger than you kid! I heard about you up there and might have tried you out, before you were hurt. But not now, NO WAY!" he explained. Henry was not a very talented football player. He wasn't very big (something new for Henry), he wasn't a gifted athlete. No, what Henry brought to the football team was simply GUTS. And he often spilled them!?! Henry loved to play football. He was defensive center and he hit the opposing linemen play after play as hard as he could! This was his place to dish out the kind of treatment he had to take from others all the time. He played hard and hit hard every play.

Henry got so involved during the games that he didn't feel any pain until after the game. He broke both hands in one game and couldn't remember when. He broke his nose and several ribs in another game, but couldn't remember when or how it happened. Henry never got his letter, he was injured most of the time. In the last season before he changed schools—he wasn't even invited out for the team. Henry missed the hitting back... he now had to hold his anger inside even in the fall... even during football season.

After he left the football coach's office Henry went to the band room. Everybody was gone except for the band director. Henry explained that he wanted to play tuba. Mr. Rodocker explained to Henry that every bandsman had to audition to get into the music program and that he already had twelve tuba players.

Henry turned toward the door as Mr. Rodocker asked: "Are you any good?"

"No, not yet, but I'll be first chair by the end of next year!" Henry replied with more hope than bravado in his voice.

"Give me three good reasons why I should let you in my band, young man," Mr. Rodocker challenged.

"No one wants to play more than I do! No one will work harder than I will! I need the music in my life and will do whatever it takes to keep it there!" Henry's arguments struck a chord with the band director. And, Henry did make first chair before the end of his junior year... just as he promised.

Henry also learned to play string bass and sang in the choir for a while. Henry had music again, and he was going to need it.

CHAPTER FOURTEEN

Henry hated his parents' parties. He always ended up being the bartender and he didn't like the way people started acting when they were drinking... and what went on later in the evenings was even worse!

There was a movie he had seen at school. His civics teacher had gotten into trouble showing it, but Henry was fascinated by it. It was called "Reefer Madness" and Henry knew what it was all about!

The parties at his parents' house would often smell sickeningly sweet like burning rope. Henry would try to escape, but somebody always cornered him and talked... or touched him for hours.

Sometimes they would give themselves shots like the doctors gave, but they didn't get healthy after the shots... they got ugly!! They would act strange and vomit and eat the vomit and drink and take their clothes off and make Henry watch as they played ugly games.

Early in one party a pretty girl only two or three years older than Henry started to talk to Henry. Susan said Henry was a handsome guy and shouldn't be so shy. She taught Henry how to do the Twist and seemed really nice. They talked and Henry told her about the music. She seemed interested and told him she was going to be a nurse like Henry's mom. Henry told her not to be like his mom.

Henry had to run to the store and get more ice. When he returned he couldn't find Susan anywhere. Henry really liked Susan. She was different.

A couple of hours later Henry went upstairs to relieve himself. As he went by his mother's bedroom he saw his step dad. He was on top of Susan. They were naked. Henry went into the bathroom, threw up and cried all night. Henry hated his parents' parties. What they all did didn't look like fun to Henry. They were all disgusting. They were all ugly. They were all mean and crazy. They all became like Henry's mother.

It was funny, but after he served the first round of drinks Henry lost his hearing. He knew music was playing in the house, but he couldn't hear any music. He just heard the noises of Hell around him.

CHAPTER FIFTEEN

Henry liked tropical fish and almost always had an aquarium. He liked to watch the colorful fish swimming around and found it very relaxing.

As Henry watched this time he noticed a commotion in a corner of the tank. Looking more closely he saw two fish fighting. As he focused on the unusual action, he noticed that he had never seen fish like these. One was rather normal looking except that it was purple in color. Henry didn't have any purple fish! The other was pre-historic looking with jagged features and a huge mouth full of curved sharp teeth! As Henry watched, the ugly green fish grabbed the hapless purple fish with his tail, which now looked more like a hand. The purple fish struggled valiantly as the water boiled and turned from clear to red and then bright white with the fury of the green fish!

Henry felt he could feel the terror of the purple fish as the green fish started eating the purple fish alive! Henry was transfixed by the image.

Suddenly Henry realized this must be a dream and remembered what he had to do to escape this horrifying scene. He yelled, "This is a dream!" The scene became the frightening, but familiar vortex. He awoke sweating and feeling more alone than ever before. This was a new dream for Henry, but soon he would have it virtually every single night at least once.

At his new high school Henry made some very good new friends maintained a three point GPA and gained the respect of the instructors and kids who got to know him. Henry was not an easy person to get close to. He seemed to always have other things on his mind... he would shrink back when touched. He was an island, an enigma, a mystery... except when playing music.

Henry was in marching band, symphonic band, orchestra, pep band, and one year also in concert band and he even sang in choir for the amount of time required to get a music major from his high school.

During one concert the orchestra was performing themes from "Exodus". The arranger wrote an absolutely beautiful solo for oboe with only a string bass accompaniment. Henry played with his very soul as Julie played the beautiful melody of pathos... and finally hope. A spotlight shone on each player, the auditorium was silent except for the inspired music played by the two young musicians. Henry fell in love with Julie during that magical moment although she would never know. Applause had never erupted at an orchestra concert during the middle of a piece before...

but it did twice on this day once in the first assembly...

and surprisingly again during the second assembly.

Henry had auditioned a few weeks earlier for a music

scholarship. He knew what he wanted to do with his

life. He would get his master's degree in music and

then conduct a small symphony orchestra and write

music for the movies. Eventually he would either have

his own commercial orchestra or conduct a major

symphony. He was never more sure of himself... or his

destination in life.

One fall night earlier in Henry's senior year he

arrived at home after a marching band practice to find

the back door locked. He searched for the key, but

could not find it. He considered the consequences of

breaking a family rule and then decided to go up on the

front porch and try to enter through the forbidden door.

On the porch he could see that there was nothing inside the house. No furniture, no people, no pictures... nothing.

He turned and left the porch and checked to make sure this was in fact the place where he had lived. It was. There was a nice elderly lady who lived next door. Henry had taken care of her lawn, shoveled her walks during the winter and kept her neat little Corvair washed and waxed for her. The lady had even encouraged Henry to take her car out for rides from time to time.

Mrs. Henderson was beside herself: "You moved today!"

"No ma'am," Henry answered.

"Yes, you moved—the moving van took everything and your parents left," she said.

"No Mrs. Henderson, I didn't move," Henry tried again to get her to understand. At that moment Henry noticed a pile of clothes and a few personal effects in a heap on the front lawn... he could tell they were his. After calming Mrs. Henderson down, Henry looked in her newspaper and found a room to rent. He called and took his stuff to his new room. Mrs. Henderson insisted on giving Henry some money. He was able to pay his first month's rent in advance. As Henry lay in his new bed that night, he tried to decide whether he was sorry or glad for the evening's happenings. He felt more alone, but he was used to that. He also realized he was no longer going to be beaten three or four times a week. He was free!

The well focused plan for his future fueled Henry. He spent even more time in the music room practicing, getting his homework done... practicing some more.

His entire world had become music... and it was beautiful!

Odd jobs and playing an occasional "gig" kept the rent paid, but there was never any money left for anything else... including food. Henry hadn't been heavy since he was in the sixth grade... although he still saw himself: "... as a fat, ugly, stupid slob." But now he was beginning to look overly thin to other people. His band director would ask Henry to go get dinner for both of them from time to time and his friends' mothers invited him to dinner often. Usually Henry would soon purge the meal after eating... he just couldn't keep anything down. He ignored these problems and kept working toward his goal, his vision of being the music.

He finally got the news that he was accepted at the University and that he was offered a full scholarship. Henry had never felt better in his entire life!

But, there was a problem. There were forms that had to be filled out. and payments that had to be made for fees and things. Henry didn't know where his mother and stepfather had gone and frankly, he didn't care... before. Now he needed his mom to fill out the forms so he could pursue his dream.

Henry went to the police. Police had always been there for Henry when he was younger. This wasn't the same department, but he was confident they would help.

Henry explained his situation... the sergeant obviously didn't believe him. A few days later he tried again. This time he talked with a juvenile officer. This time he was believed, but the officer kept asking questions about where Henry was living and who was responsible for him. These questions made Henry very nervous.

Finally a call came in and the officer wrote down the address of Henry's mom. They had moved to another part of the state. Henry scribbled the address down in his notebook and left when the officer left the room to get some sort of "counselor".

Henry had spent his last few coins on postage to send the papers to his mother. He wrote a nice letter explaining the process and that it would cost her nothing. He waited for her reply.

Henry's grades were even better this last semester. He had 6 A's and a C at mid term, but worked hard enough in economics to raise that grade to an A for final grades! He was very nervous, but performed well at his required recital. During the recital Henry could not see the audience. He was sure a couple of teachers and a few friends were there... and maybe some of their parents, but he was embarrassed that there would be no family, and that the audience was so tiny. After the last number was rendered Henry felt funny and nearly passed out while taking his bow. As the lights came down on the stage and up in the auditorium, Henry saw that the audience was not small like he expected, but huge! It seemed everybody in the music department, their parents, and all his other teachers from the past two years were there! Henry forgot how horrible he felt. Henry was once again assured that his choice for his life's work was right.

It was a beautiful spring morning when Henry got the envelope he had been waiting for. He didn't open it... he would save it for school. There was an Easter Assembly that day and Henry would play the continuo part for Bach's Easter Cantata two times in a row for both assemblies. He wanted to work on a few measures that were awkward for him to play. After he had practiced for an hour, other kids began arriving in the music room.

Henry opened the envelope as he walked through the band room. When he saw the contents of the envelope his heart stopped... then the air turned red and then white with rage. Through the doorway in front of him came a sophomore... Robby was one of Henry's tuba students and although they didn't hang around together, most people would say they were friends.

In the heat of his rage Henry struck out at the first target he saw. The upper cut to Robby's chin raised him off his feet and propelled him over a couple of people who were bending over their instrument cases and into a heap against the far wall. As this happened

113

the door to Henry's right opened and through it came Mr. Rodocker. The band director grabbed Henry and escorted him into his office slamming the door behind them. Seeing the envelope in Henry's hand he opened it and saw the contents. He didn't stop Henry as he walked out and over to the cowering Robby to apologize: "I'm so sorry, Robby!

Please forgive me, I got some bad news this morning... I'm so sorry..."

"It's OK, man. I'd hate to have you mad at me!" Robby said while mopping his bleeding jaw.

The envelope contained the forms Henry had sent to be signed. Instead of signatures there were expletives written all over the forms and they were torn like the person doing the writing was holding the pen in their fist instead of their fingers. The music was gone again.

CHAPTER SIXTEEN

The fish dream was on Henry's mind constantly now. He would doodle it absentmindedly in his notes or in his textbooks. Henry had moved back to his hometown to go to a Junior College with a good reputation. Henry was taking general courses and trying to decide what compromise to take. He hadn't had the opportunity or inclination to play tuba since the night he graduated, but he played string bass and electric bass in dance bands and rock groups in town. He felt like a musical prostitute. Not because he didn't like to listen to the kind of music he was playing four or more nights a week, but because he was playing for money. The music was OK, but he never became a part of it anymore. He worked other jobs, too. Bell Hop, Stock Clerk, Night Auditor... his resume was growing.

He had made more friends... and some of the parents of those friends really liked Henry. He liked them, too. Two of his friends had been adopted... Henry wished he had been adopted. He was envious of the bonds of love that were wrapped softly around his friends.

Henry's grades were pretty good especially considering he was working two jobs, plus the playing, and carrying more than what was considered to be a full load of classes each semester. Once again his talents had made him more visible, than he wanted to be.

He was the announcer and occasional singer in a dance band. He was editor of the college newspaper with a column that was as popular as it was controversial… and it seemed like "female types" (how he referred to girls) were more interested in him than he was comfortable to be around them. Henry would study all night many nights, not because he wanted to, but because he knew if he would allow himself to sleep he would have more of the fish nightmares. Each time he had the dream, it would last longer, be more graphic and be more terrifying. He wasn't sure he wanted to know what the dream meant, but he was about to find out! The lecturer was a Ph.D. from the university to which Henry was once headed. The psychologist was talking about the relationship between students and teachers. After the lecture the speaker joined a group of psychology students in the Union.

"Whose text is this?" inquired the professor.

"It's mine," replied Henry.

"May I look at it?"

"Sure!"

"I helped the author write this text and... what is this??!" he suddenly noticed Henry's doodles. "Young man what are these? Are they depicting dreams?"

"Yeah, sure," Henry choked.

"What do they mean, Dr. Foster?" chorused the group minus Henry. "I don't know this young man, but this is a classic!" said Dr. Foster. "Is this the same dream over and over? Is it in color? How do you feel about it? Please tell me," he continued.

"Yes, I have it several times a week. Sometimes several times in one night. The big fish is bright green and the little one is purple," Henry reluctantly explained already wishing he was anywhere else.

"Young man, you are frightened by women; aren't you?"

Henry couldn't speak.

CHAPTER SEVENTEEN

Henry was known for doing crazy things! He was a demon on water skis, dove from highway bridges into the water below... some times very shallow water... and would ride on the roof of cars—especially if the driver had a "female type" in the car.

Henry also tried to enlist in the Navy, Marines, and Air Force and was rejected by all. His x-rays were notorious! When he graduated from junior college he was already to continue his education to become an English teacher... if he could get the money together before the deadline. Henry had spent months sleeping in the lobby of the hotel he occasionally worked at... or, out in the street on several nights. He finally rented a room from his father. The house was rented

119

downstairs by a drunk and his unfortunate son. The upstairs was unfinished, but Henry could work off some of the rent.

For graduation from JC, his grandfather had given him some money. With it he put a down payment down on a little motorcycle.

Viet Nam had heated up as Henry predicted it would in a speech he gave in freshman speech class. That speech got him suspended for three days. And, hung a "radical" label on him.

Because all his friends were getting drafted, it was hard to keep a band together and money was becoming a bigger problem. One night Henry was riding his motorcycle after work and deciding if he should get going real fast and run head-on into a semi or not. Henry thought about suicide a lot. He was sure nobody would ever notice that he had ever darkened the earth with his presence. He was almost sure that suicide was the answer when a girl he knew from school flagged him down. He wasn't sure why he stopped, but it was obvious she was crying.

She asked for some change to call her parents on the pay phone. Henry gave her a dollar's worth of change and started to leave when she asked him to wait for her. For some reason he didn't know—he waited.

He didn't think about the day being the Fourth of July, but while on their ride they stopped to watch when they saw the fireworks.

Sharon had long reddish hair and looked like a typical "child of the 60's". She was not unattractive, but she wouldn't be noticed in a crowd, either. The only thing Henry remembered about her was that she was the one who dropped the venetian blinds on his head before a class they were both in. Sharon said she wasn't tired and not ready to go back to her place. Henry said he had to get home and she said that was fine with her. They talked all night.

When Henry got home from work the next night Sharon was there. They talked all night.

When Henry got home the next evening she was there again. They talked all night.

The next day Henry had off. He intended to go to his favorite beach and spend the day. Sharon invited herself along. That evening Henry dropped Sharon off and went to a movie. When he got home after the movie Sharon was there on the steps to his apartment crying.

Henry asked what was wrong. Sharon responded by saying that it seemed that afternoon Henry had failed to pick up on her "signals". "I was standing there, naked, and you didn't even notice!" she was nearly screaming at this point. "Look at me, damn it!!" she said as she bared her self to the frightened young man with her.

A similar thing had happened to Henry a few months before. A friend he worked with asked Henry to help her with homework and ended up offering a course in biology Henry was NOT ready to pursue. Then the rumors started. Was Henry a "Queer?" Sharon was yelling at Henry to do something and asked him if he was a faggot. Henry knew he didn't like men sexually, but he wasn't sure he liked women either!?!?! He had vague memories of being fondled by his mother and her drunken friends when he was very young. And, of being forced to spend nights in his mother's bed when she was alone and way passed the time Henry wanted to be there. The air turned red, then white and Henry was in his nightmare. He asked again and again if this was a dream... but it didn't work. This was real and Henry was really being consumed.

"Hey you're pretty good," Sharon said a while later. "You really were afraid, weren't you?"

Henry could not answer. He just cried inside. When Henry felt this bad, he would remember some of the music he used to play. This would always make him feel better. But, this night the music wouldn't come to him... even in his memory. Six stormy years later he was single again.

CHAPTER EIGHTEEN

Henry had decided to sub-let his rented house to his new secretary. She was pregnant and her husband had just lost his job. Henry let them have his house for an amount he knew they could afford. He kept paying the landlady the full amount of the rent.

The day Henry decided to look for an apartment so his secretary and her husband could move in would change his life again.

As he started to leave the office on his lunch hour, he told Elaine that he would be late returning because he was going to look at some apartments. Elaine was the most beautiful woman he had ever seen! She had beautiful long legs, long blonde hair that she could sit on and a very pretty face and smile. She was the secretary for the President of the company and she sat in for the regular receptionist at lunch hour.

Elaine asked Henry if he could delay his excursion so she could look at apartments, too. She and Henry had been friends and he even helped her with some business and personal problems, but he didn't ever dare fantasize about such a gorgeous woman!

When they had looked at the first apartment they returned to the rental office. Henry wasn't even sure he was going to like apartment living and was thinking about alternatives when the apartment complex manager asked the question: "Well, what do you think?"

Elaine said without hesitating, "We'll take it!" Henry's heart began pounding, he was shaking as he picked up the pen and signed the lease. He moved in that Saturday. Elaine moved in the next day.

Within a few months they were married in Chicago after escaping a major fire in their hotel. They kept their marriage secret for a while because of all the things they knew about the company they worked for, but eventually the rumors were so bad, Henry announced that they had been married. Most of the people who worked for him were very happy for the couple and his boss even gave them a congratulatory card, which was definitely NOT expected from him of all people!

Eventually they had a nice home, great jobs and the two most wonderful children ever created.

CHAPTER NINETEEN

Over the years Henry learned a lot about life. He learned that STRESS is a long horizontal tunnel. Sometimes you can see the light at the end of the tunnel, but often you can't. Henry spent a lot of time in the dark.

His beautiful wife wanted nice things and Henry worked hard to get them for her. But, he was tired and something was missing... he didn't know what. After a few years of disappointing her again and again, she decided to move on. Henry had been so afraid this was going to happen. He saw everything he ever wanted going away. He couldn't concentrate on his business and it began to shrink. He decided to give everything to her for his kids. She kept talking about leaving the state and moving so far Henry wouldn't see his kids grow up or be a part of their lives.

The only place Henry felt alive was on his motorcycle. He loved his bike and treated it like a piece of art. One day while riding fast out in the country the horizontal tunnel that was STRESS turned vertical! Henry saw the trees ahead of him and decided to get out of the way so his family could move ahead without him holding them back. At the last minute he changed his mind and turned backed onto the road. He wasn't sure why.

The arrangements for the divorce were being discussed, but Henry couldn't talk about it and left in the middle of most of the conversations. Or, even worse, he would try to change her mind.

That night in the two-room cottage Henry rented from the family to keep his paternal grandmother in a home for the aged; Henry lost his grip on the sides of the vertical tunnel of depression. As he fell he made the decision that the world would be a much better place if he wasn't in it. After all, he never fit in anywhere. He never felt a part of a family... nor did he understand what love was... except that he loved his children, and his dog. But, then they would forget him, he was no good for them anyway... he was just a complication in their lives. Someone who brought discomfort and trouble to them. He was responsible for all the sadness in the lives of those he loved and wanted to love him in return. His kids and that dog seemed to love him, but they didn't know any better... they would change, everyone else did... no, there was only one honorable thing to do. Henry remembered what he had heard about people who cut their wrists. They aren't serious if they cut across their wrist he had heard a policeman say once. You had to cut along the vertical dimension of the arm, parallel to the bones and ligaments so the arteries would be cut.

He felt like he was free-falling in this tunnel, there was no light above and everything was silent. He thought that it was like he was falling into a "well of souls" even though it was silent, it was as though he could hear the moans of other tortured beings.

The silent sound of the screams of the tortured was deafening. He tried to remember his favorite movie theme... he couldn't. He tried to remember the last number he had ever played on the tuba, but he remembered nothing... heard nothing but the horrible silent sounds of suffering, pain, loneliness.

As he cut his flesh the expected pain wasn't there. "You see, this is the right thing to do," he thought to himself. "All the pain is going to go away... and all the pain I have been inflicting on others will be gone, too,"

he said out loud knowing there was no one to hear him.

Other times when he had thought about doing this, he

imagined being found by his mother, wife or

whomever depending upon the time in his life that he

tried to leave. BUT this time he wasn't thinking about

anyone... or anything but the pain of being so alone...

so fat, so ugly, so evil, so clumsy, so stupid and so

worthless. He had never found his place on this earth...

maybe he would find it now.

CHAPTER TWENTY

"Deputy," the German Shepherd, was a Father's Day gift. He and Henry's daughter were puppies together. Deputy was a very intelligent dog. Henry had watched one day as the dog knocked his daughter aside as she was about to be hit by a car while Henry was too far away... helpless and unable to reach his daughter in time.

Deputy was also a baby monitor. When Henry's son was a baby, he would have trouble breathing sometimes at night. Deputy would wake Henry and tug on his arm and lead him to his son's bed. Henry would pick up his son and take him into the living room and let him sleep on Henry's chest... Deputy would sleep next to them.

Deputy liked to ride and was often with Henry at the office or on calls. Henry's clients all liked the dog, too. During the period that led to Henry's moving out, SHE had decided and Henry agreed that Deputy should stay with his kids. The children loved their dog and he obviously loved them back. But Deputy just wasn't happy there and would jump in Henry's car and not get out when Henry visited. It got harder and harder to remove the dog from the car before Henry left.

Henry stayed away for a while as requested by his soon to be ex spouse. During that time Deputy stopped eating and wouldn't play much with his kids. Finally, it was clear to everyone that Deputy should be with Henry.

As the blood drained out of Henry's arm and he lost consciousness, the last thing Henry saw was the face of his dog.

The next morning Henry awoke weakly. He was soon aware that he and his dog were attached. Deputy had stood next to his master all night leaning against the bleeding wounds. Henry began to cry as the dog licked his face. After he separated himself from the dog and dressed his wounds Henry called his best human friend and asked for help.

His friend told him that Henry had to get in touch with professional help and that he would call back to make sure Henry had done it. Henry dialed the number of his family doctor. When he was put on hold there was music. It was a favorite movie theme. The doctor referred him to a psychiatrist and later his friend drove him to the place where the healing would start.

CHAPTER TWENTY-ONE

The room was featureless. Just two beds, two cabinets and nothing else. There was no roommate, but obviously there could be. The strip inspection had just ended with the "jailer" making notes. Henry could not believe he was here.

Everything seemed surreal. The smells, the sounds… it was like he wasn't really there. It was like he was not really anywhere!

Waking up attached to his dog was a major surprise. Calling his friend and then his doctor and then the psychiatrist seemed like they happened to somebody else. The appointment with the psychiatrist was almost enough to change his mind. The admission procedure was pretty typical, but when the big doors closed behind him he was very aware of what he had done.

He planned to be there a couple of days... it sounded like they planned for him to be around awhile longer. The other patients were in the "smoke room"... Henry wanted no part of that place or those people. He was different. They couldn't possibly understand how he felt or why he was there.

Henry had hit the bottom... or so he thought. This was the "nut house", the "loony bin", the "mental institution"... the worst place on this earth. His mother was right. Henry was a "nut case"! He was proving he is the "psychotic bastard" she always told him he was. This was proof!

He remembered all her descriptions of mental institutions and felt the terror of her warnings to him. He had "screwed up" big time! This was the ultimate failure. He could hear his mother laughing at him. Damn! She was right! He couldn't sleep… he wished he had not bungled his suicide attempt. He looked around the room for a weapon to use against himself. He held his breath… but he couldn't stop the life force within him. Something inside him wouldn't let him give up. It wasn't very strong, but it was there. Henry hated it! He hated where he was and what he had become.

"What is happiness? Why can't I have a little? Why am I losing everything again? God, what did I do to deserve my life?! Please, please, help me… help me die… please…" Henry lost awareness from the exhaustion of the situation… it wasn't sleep, but he wasn't crying… nor were there nightmares – where he was and the situation was nightmare enough.

The next morning began with a meeting with his doctor. He could barely understand the doctor. He was foreign and didn't seem to care whether Henry understood him or not. He prescribed medications. Henry protested, but the doctor ignored him. This was typical.

Next was group therapy. Henry had never seen a room with more weird people! There must be some mistake? How can this be the right group?? The psychologist who led these sessions explained that he would be there every other day and that another guy would take the opposite days. This guy was tough! He made people in the group talk whether they wanted to talk or not.

Henry dreaded the time he would have to talk. When it was his turn he said: "I'm not sure why I'm here... to get better I guess." That seemed to be enough and they went on to the next person. After a while things got kind of interesting, but Henry chose not to participate.

Next was occupational therapy! They decided Henry would do ceramics. Henry chose a ceramic nut to finish... it seemed appropriate to him.

There were a lot of tests. Some seemed like I. Q. tests. Some were obviously designed to uncover weird stuff!

Late in the afternoon Henry was told to meet a psychologist at a certain room. He was told this was individual therapy.

When Margaret opened the door Henry was surprised to see that she was a very attractive lady. "This seems like hospital logic to me," he said.

"What do you mean?" answered the freckled and red headed lady across the desk.

"I mean that I have problems with women and then my psychologist is a woman. This seems a little strange to me, that's all," explained Henry.

"You can choose another psychologist if you want. But why don't you give me a chance first. It could be the thing you need most is the same thing you fear most," she said as Henry relaxed — just a little, after all, he had to keep his guard up!

"I've invited your wife to come in, Henry," said Margaret.

"She won't come," assured Henry.

"I need to get to know you in every way I can, Henry. And besides, I can be very persuasive," continued Margaret.

It was several sessions later that Margaret reported that she had finally actually talked with Henry's wife.

"Henry, there is no chance for reconciliation. Your wife is not very cooperative is she? Why did you marry her, Henry," she continued.

After Henry had explained the strange way he had gotten together with the mother of his children, and then the equally odd way he had gotten together with his first wife… his psychologist said she saw a pattern and asked Henry if he did, too.

In one session Henry was told that his tests revealed that he was a genius. Henry balked at that idea, but Margaret said that the battery of tests were quite reliable. She also explained that their conversations had led her to some treatment decisions and preliminary conclusions.

She explained that Henry's problems with women were the result of his problems with his mother. She asked if Henry ever heard his mother talking to him?

"I'm not like those other people! I haven't heard God talking to me... or, voices telling me to do dumb things!" he paused. "Yes, sometimes."

Henry explained that every time he failed, or worried about failing he heard the voice of his mother telling him how worthless he was and that he would never amount to anything. As the sessions continued he began hearing those words on purpose.

CHAPTER TWENTY-TWO

Henry began to learn about the hospital. He learned how to "work the system" so he could get out of there.

First, he started going into the "smoke room" and making friends with the other patients. The guards treated him a lot different when he started doing that. He started going on the group outings in the evening. It was strange, but he realized he felt kind of uncomfortable on these outings!

One day they started biofeedback therapy, on Henry. He was afraid it was "shock therapy" at first! He was ready to get the heck out of there, but the guards finally explained what was going to happen. Henry made the needles do what he wanted them to do. After all, Henry had practiced self-control all his life.

As a kid he could hold his breath for several minutes… sit on the bottom of the lake or a pool and stuff like that. This was no big deal. They didn't like what Henry was doing though and they never asked him to do it again.

After a while he asked for and was granted a pass. This was one of the things people did before they left.

He spent a Sunday with his father, stepmother and stepbrother and half sisters and their families. It was not a very pleasant experience and his doctor and the psychologists talked about what happened on that pass a lot for the next few sessions.

Henry started trying to show a different attitude to the guards. In ceramics Henry did busts of his favorite composers planning to send them to his daughter, then he did some kitchen items for his half sister and eventually he took on a major ceramic challenge. The cookie jar he worked on for weeks and weeks was like a pile of fruit and it would turn out impressively.

Other things Henry learned included better ways to hide his meds. The best way was to wait until he took his shower dissolving them as they went down the drain. A couple of times the guards paid too much attention to him so he had to take the damned pills, but during the months he was in the hospital, that only happened two or three times. Henry hated pills... he knew what that junk could do to people. He wanted to make sure his thoughts and actions were HIM, not some character created by chemicals!

He also learned that some pretty nice... if troubled people came to the hospital. In fact Henry had a room mate for a while that he liked a lot. They remain casual friends to this day.

What Henry learned one day in group was a shock, though.

The group psychologists were playing games with the group. One guy was a good guy. His sessions were easy. He wouldn't make you talk if you didn't want to and never said anything that somebody said was dumb. The whole group liked Bill.

Jack was a different story! He challenged the group. He made every one talk and he would call bullshit... bullshit!

People would come and go from the group. Sometimes the patients would leave the hospital, but many times they would just change to a different group.

This particular day Henry was the only man in a group of women. Jack started the session and then stopped. Everybody was listening to the silence when he said, "This is an unusual group. This is the first time we have ever had a group where every member had been sexually abused…"

Every eye in the room turned to look at Henry. Henry was the only one who noticed Bill had entered the room and through the door he briefly saw the staff listening at the door.

Henry didn't know what to do or say. He wanted to argue with Jack, but something kept him from doing that. The women in the room all moved toward Henry making him very uncomfortable. Then they started crying. Henry started crying, too. The next hour was basically everyone crying. After the session a couple of the women gave Henry a hug. Hospital rules were patients could touch you, but staff couldn't!

Henry didn't say much of anything to anyone for the rest of the afternoon. He almost wished that

Margaret would "stand him up" as she occasionally did. When she stood him up she often would see him at other times… but not always. Henry figured it was part of the mind games they played at the sanitarium.

When Margaret arrived she said they were going to do something different. She called it regression therapy. She made Henry imagine he was going back in time. She didn't hypnotize Henry, but something was going on. Henry even sounded different as he spoke!? Then, he started describing some things he and his mother did that he had not thought about — ever! These were things that he knew he would die if he said out loud!

BUT, he was saying them… and he wasn't dying.

Henry realized what he was saying and asked to stop. Then, he asked to leave the hospital… then, he grabbed the door knob. At that moment Margaret put her arms around Henry and they both broke down in tears. They wept together for over an hour. Then they visited Henry at other ages. He told about the mop handle, being locked in the attic, how ugly he was and how that's when he first wanted to die.

He told about lying on the highway. He told about doing crazy stunts and hoping he could save someone's life and die doing it. He described beating after beating and each blow hurt him as he talked about it. The pains that he had been holding back for years and years were all coming at the same time! Margaret held his hand as he talked. Then exhausted she asked if he was hungry. When he said no… she said she was and she called for a couple of trays. It was then that Henry realized that it was the next day. He had been talking with Margaret for over twelve hours.

After eating they talked for another three and a half hours. Henry faced and talked to every Henry at every age making peace and telling him that all the things his mother and other people had told him were lies.

There was one Henry that he just couldn't face. That was the Henry who had been locked in the attic. Henry thought that Henry was ugly and stupid and deserved what he got. Margaret tried to change Henry's mind, but it didn't work. It was like that part of him was a dead issue. There was simply no reason to discuss it.

CHAPTER TWENTY-THREE

Henry continued to learn about the hospital and about depression.

One of the new patients went from the room with leather wallpaper... a room Henry was very proud to have never been in... to buying new paddles for the ping pong table! This guy kept saying there was nothing wrong with him.

He knew exactly what to say and do. Henry figured George had been in the hospital before. Henry found out George was a school principal. A job Henry had wanted to have. George had a beautiful wife and very nice children and they always visited every day during visiting hours. No one visited Henry.

Henry was a little jealous of George. He had everything Henry wanted but couldn't have. Still, there was something about George. Being a model patient, George was out of there in just a few days.

Henry talked to everybody about letting George go. Henry said George hadn't dealt with anything. Henry said it was criminal to let him go! The staff told Henry that George… even Henry could walk out of there at any time. Henry was surprised by that statement. One of the hospital games that he hadn't figured out yet was that the big doors didn't lock… they just looked like they did, and the staff was very good at keeping up the charade!

It was morning again. Henry had slept about two hours like he usually did and lay in his bed the rest of the night waiting for the dawn… as he usually did. That morning the staff all looked more depressed than the patients. Henry asked, but nobody would explain. They wouldn't let anyone watch TV that morning for a while either. Something weird was happening.

That afternoon in his session with Margaret, Henry mentioned George and how concerned he was that George hadn't worked on his problems and that the staff let him go when it was obvious he wasn't OK!

Margaret looked like she was about to cry, "Henry, George hung himself yesterday and his wife found him last night." The session was over. Henry just left.

Henry had thought a lot about suicide. His cuts had healed weeks before, but he couldn't stop thinking about how it felt. He read some books that Jack and Margaret let him read about depression and suicide. Henry developed his own theory about the method people chose to end their lives. In later years his theories would solidify, but that's another story.

People who took pills wanted to be caught and saved. They didn't really want to end their lives... only to get attention. They were screaming out in their pain!

People who gassed themselves, shot themselves, or crashed their cars were cowards, but determined cowards. They didn't want to be stopped and didn't think at all about anyone but themselves. This was the ultimate way to run away from their problems.

People who burned themselves wanted to make a big statement. They wanted the whole world to know about their pain... and to feel badly about what they (the world) made them do.

People who chose hanging were punishing someone. They knew they would be found and planned who would find them. "That will teach them!" was their final thought no doubt.

People who impaled them selves or cut their wrists were the loneliest people of all. They weren't screaming to be stopped, or planning to be found, they weren't making any major statements or punishing anybody. No, people who cut just had given up on their ability to contribute to the world. They were convinced that the world, their loved-ones, everybody… would be better off without them around. This was the ultimate act of depression! There was no light in the hole… these people had learned that there is no bottom to the "well of souls"… no bottom to the vertical hole of depression. Free falling in that hole was fatal! Hope is of the light… faith is seeing the light… depression is being convinced the light will never shine for them again. Depression is feeling that it is a sin to let the light shine on them.

CHAPTER TWENTY-FOUR

Getting better is work! Playing the hospital game was a battle. You could never let down your guard or the staff was there to notice and write it down! More than once Henry figured he was on his way out… only to violate some rule and be "written up"!

The sessions with Margaret were the best therapy. The other therapies were helpful, but the real work was going on in those sessions.

One day Margaret asked Henry if he wanted to go for a walk? "Leave the hospital? Isn't that against the rules?" queried Henry.

"Sure, but let's do it anyway! It is a beautiful day, Henry, and you haven't been outside except to go on group recreation in weeks," she continued.

Henry had begun to feel more comfortable inside the hospital than outside! The staff seemed to like Henry... something he wasn't used to. The people he met inside were all like him. He had something in common with each of them. They were like... well, like family, kind of.

On their walk Margaret asked Henry a lot of questions about what he was going to do after he left the hospital. Henry was a little startled at first. He hadn't thought about leaving the hospital. He had so much more work to do... and...."Henry, how do you feel right this minute?" asked Margaret.

Henry had dreaded that question when she first started asking it months before. She would always tell him to "get in touch with his feelings". Along the way he had "gotten in touch" all right!! Henry had felt all the feelings possible except one.

He answered without any noticeable hesitation, "I feel wonderful, but a little uncomfortable."

"What is uncomfortable?" she asked.

"It is almost like I was standing here naked… yeah, that's it — naked… that's how I feel!" Henry explained.

"Why do you feel naked, Henry?" she asked.

Henry went on to explain that he felt that he was no longer protected… that he couldn't hide any more and that everything anyone could possibly know about him… everybody knew.

Margaret reminded Henry that not everybody knew all the details and then she let Henry continue.

Henry talked about how he had always felt tougher than everyone else… different than everyone else… kind of untouchable before he started getting better. Now he felt no walls between himself and the world.

159

"You look like you're open to anything and everything, Henry. I'm very happy and proud to know you, Henry. I have never met anyone who worked so hard. You had a lot to overcome, but Henry I believe you're on your way," she said with a smile.

"Henry, you are a charming, intelligent, caring man. Some woman is going to make you very happy," she continued.

"Oh NO! Not me!… I've had it with women. They only mean pain for me!" he protested.

"Do I hurt you, Henry? Do I scare you?"

"Well, no, but you're different," he said.

"Henry, start looking around you. There is a person… probably dozens… who will help you finish what we… really you have started," Margaret explained.

"I don't think so!"

"Well, Henry, we've done all we can for you. You know all you need to know and know how to go the rest of the way on your own. I'm recommending that you be discharged."

Henry was pleased and a little frightened. Yes, he was feeling frightened. He hadn't felt really frightened since he was a very young child. He had learned how to not be afraid... but in learning that, he had forgotten how to love and be loved.

The healing would continue – "a work in progress" as he would often describe it... but it would be years before Henry would face the little boy in the attic. It would be years before someone so wonderful would recognize that child and bring him back to life. It would be years before Henry learned how to fall in love.

An end, but also a new beginning...

CHAPTER TWENTY-FIVE

It was a beautiful spring day and Henry was on his way to a business meeting in a city not too far from Port City where he used to live. Henry loved the car he was driving. It was the first he had ever had with a cassette tape deck. He was listening to movie soundtrack music by his favorite composer Henry Mancini.

He had gone through this particular small town hundreds of times over the years. He had noticed the large cemetery every time, but something was different this day.

As he slowed at the city limits he turned into the cemetery. He didn't decide to turn, he just turned and turned off the music.

It had been twenty years since his mother had died and his last conversation with her was an ugly argument. He went to his mother's funeral, but didn't go to the burial afterwards. He wasn't sure where she had been buried, but his step-father's family was from that little town so it was somewhat logical that she might be buried there.

He drove around looking for the grave for a half hour or so. Noticing the time, he decided this was a dumb idea and that he didn't even know if she was buried there anyway.

Giving up on his quest he turned his car down one of the dirt pathways and was almost back to the highway when coming over a slight hill he saw a tractor with several lawn mowers hanging off the back and sides of the strange looking machine. It was obvious the driver would have a major problem pulling off the path, so Henry put his car in reverse and backed up about a quarter of a mile to an intersection with room for the tractor to turn.

The tractor driver stopped in Henry's way and came over to the car.

"Thank you for backing up! I wasn't sure how to get off the path in that old part of the cemetery without running over one of the headstones," explained the caretaker. "Can I do anything for you?"

"Well, I was looking for a grave, but couldn't find it," Henry explained.

"What's the name?" asked the caretaker.

"Mrs. Gwendolyn Darling is the name," Henry replied and as he said it, the irony of his step father and mother's name struck him again as it had years before.

"When did she pass away? We have some up on the hill and some down by the road in the new section of the cemetery," the older man asked.

"Nineteen sixty-seven," replied Henry.

"Oh, they're up on the hill… let me show you," the caretaker said as Henry and he walked up another path. "There they are. Thanks again for your help down there," the caretaker said as he walked away.

"You're very welcome! Thanks for your help, too!" Henry said.

Over the years Henry had dreamed and fantasized about things he wanted to do to defile his mother's grave. Now he was standing there looking at the headstone but his feelings were not at all what he imagined they would be.

He began to talk to the slab of granite and the grass around it. "Mom, I do not in any way condone what you did to me or yourself! I think you chose to be a very evil and hateful person. BUT, I want to thank you for making me the person that I am. I am strong! I know what is right and what paths to walk in my life. I've become almost the exact opposite of you in every way. I do want to thank you for giving me your sense of design and style and your love for colors. I do want to thank you for showing me all the things NOT to do in life. I do want to thank you for teaching me self reliance and self discipline," Henry said to the small unglamorous headstone.

He stood at the grave and stared at the name carved in the marble as if memorizing it. He stood for several minutes before he resumed his conversation with the ground. "I want to apologize for never living up to your expectations and not always being the kind of son I wanted to be. I want to apologize for my contributions to the argument we had the last time we spoke. Even though you were way out of line in your accusations, I am a bigger man than that and I should not have let you engage me in your ugly game."

He started to turn and walk away, but he realized he wasn't finished: "I want you to know that I will always be your son and that I love you for that." A single tear formed in his eye and ran down his cheek. He continued, "This is my final notice that you are dead and that I will not listen to your voice any more… good bye, mother."

Henry turned and walked back to his car. As he walked he noticed the beautiful flowers on some of the graves. They were more beautiful than he had ever seen before… in fact the sky was brighter and the song of the birds was sweeter than it had ever seemed before.

Henry felt an entirely new feeling. It was a little like the big lake at dawn... calm and flat like a huge mirror. It was like soft music or a watercolor painting. It was kind of beautiful and peaceful. He felt as if a final barrier had been blasted away, like he truly was naked... and he liked feeling that way. He felt about one hundred and five pounds was no longer on his shoulders... a burden had been lifted from him. He thought about things religious. He missed his children and a couple of special friends. He wanted to tell them about what had just happened. He suddenly felt like he had been missing something important in his life. He promised himself he would start that very day to determine what he was missing and how to get it. He realized he was smiling.

About The Author

Larry works for the Chamber of Commerce in his hometown. He is a positive person with passions for good causes; active in workforce development efforts and influencing educational institutions to reform with a new focus on work skills, the work ethic, and making education relevant.

Larry's career has been in communications. He writes a monthly column in a popular city magazine. He is also a musician, playing tuba in several concert bands and his own brass quartet, and is an avid collector of toys.

His life was a struggle at times, but he is now recognized for his truly positive attitude and his belief in people.